OPENING THE BIBLE

Thomas Merton
OPENING THE BIBLE

With an Introduction by Rob Stone

The Liturgical Press
Collegeville, Minnesota

Fortress Press
Philadelphia, Pennsylvania

Library of Congress Cataloging-in-Publication Data

Merton, Thomas, 1915–1968.
   Opening the Bible.

   Includes bibliographical references.
      1. Bible—Criticism, interpretation, etc.   I. Title.
BS511.2.M47   1986   220.6'1   85-24722
ISBN 0-8006-1910-2
ISBN 0-8146-0408-0 (Liturgical Press)

OPENING THE BIBLE

Introduction

In December, 1966, rabbi and biblical scholar Abraham Heschel telephoned Thomas Merton at the Abbey of Gethsemani regarding a writing project for Time-Life Books. The news reached Merton second-hand and caused some confusion. But while he was "not too happy with big fancy projects organized by the mass media,"[1] Merton was still interested in finding out more.

The monk was soon at work on an introductory essay, entitled "Opening the Bible," for an edition of the Bible to be published by Time-Life. For some reason the project fell through in 1967. But by September of that year Merton had produced an outline, and then by Advent a draft (heavily corrected with inserts and additions in hand), of "Opening the Bible." The manuscript is now in the possession of the Thomas Merton Studies Center of Bellarmine College, Louisville, Kentucky.

It is apparent that Merton approached this writing with some trepidation, saying, "I sincerely doubt my capacity to write anything worthwhile on the Bible. I am not a pro."[2] Despite these misgivings, a reading of the essay shows it to be an excellent example of the author's mature theological reflections—and his sense of humor.

Merton is quick to point out that the Bible, "a dangerous book" for which "all blurbs are impossible," can outrage, affront, perplex, or even bore its readers. And, he observes, some readers of the word of God find it easier to involve themselves in television commercials than in the Bible!

And what is this "word of God?" It is not an artificial system of thou shall or thou shalt not which demands blind acceptance. Rather, it is a word of liberating and transforming power. The basis of this power is the Bible's ability to answer the question "What is this book?" with another: "Who is this that reads it?" The message of the Bible is bound up with determining the true identity of its reader, a process which includes identifying God and entering into a reciprocal relationship with him.

If we cease questioning the Bible, and aren't questioned by it, Merton warns, then perhaps our reading of it is no longer serious. This questioning stance of the Bible makes it possible for even the unbeliever to discover new aspects of its message. But the Bible demands the reader's personal involvement. Because such involvement lays one open to unforseen conclusions, our tendency is to avoid the arguments which lie within its pages altogether, particularly when we have predetermined what the Bible will say to us!

Merton builds on this foundation by interweaving the Bible's witness to the power it contains with the effect it has had on people who read it "outside the official framework of belief." He cites the works of the latter, including the Italian cinematographer Pasolini, psychoanalyst Erich Fromm, and novelist William Faulkner, as examples of serious responses to the Bible's message.

This essay was written in an urgent day: the one in which we live is no less fraught with spiritual and temporal dangers. Even now, Thomas Merton urges us to reject looking to the Bible for "sure-fire methods for individual rescue from the world." Instead, we must read it with discernment to respond decisively to the challenges of an unpredictable age.

Robert E. Stone, II
Ann Arbor, Michigan
October, 1985

1. Letter to Abraham Heschel, December 12, 1966. *Thomas Merton. The Hidden Ground of Love. Letters.* Selected and edited by William H. Shannon. (New York: Farrar, Straus, Giroux, 1985) 435.

2. *Ibid.*

"What kind of book is this?" Such a question cannot be answered without taking into account the very peculiar claims that have been made for the Bible by Christian, Jewish and even Muslim believers: claims which, to many modern men, are outrageous. Claims that this book is unlike any other, and that man's very destiny depends on it.

We cannot understand anything about the Bible unless we face the fact that these claims are made seriously, and that the outrage taken at them is also fully serious. Neither can be discounted. It is of the very nature of the Bible to affront, perplex and astonish the human mind. Hence the reader who opens the Bible must be prepared for disorientation, confusion, incomprehension, perhaps outrage.

The Bible is without question one of the most unsatisfying books ever written—at least until the reader has come to terms with it in a very special way. But it is a difficult book to come to terms with. Far easier, perhaps, if one just *pretends* the question is all settled in advance: one hears from others that this is a "Sacred Book," takes their word for it, and resolves not to get involved. Let them read it in the churches: we respect them for it, and we respect their book. But above all let it be *their* book! We will let "them" read it and perhaps at times we will respectfully listen to their reading. We might even go so far as to read a little of it with them, in the way "they"

11

read it. And so, from the start, we tend to take a curiously alienated stand with regard to the Bible—even when we are believers. We approach the Bible cautiously, taking into account the claims that are made for it by others. And the claims cannot be ignored. But they are the claims *of others*, who tell us what we ourselves need before we have a chance to determine our own needs and formulate our own questions. And they tell us what the Bible demands of us before the Bible itself has a chance to make known its own claims.

However, we should not consider ourselves obliged to accept *all* official or sectarian claims uncritically. As a matter of fact, we should be courageously ready to distinguish between the claims which believers make for the Bible and the perhaps even greater claims they make for *themselves*, because of the Bible. Obviously, this is not the place to discuss the latter. It is enough to take account of their existence, and to admit that believers tend to surround the Bible with even greater problems than it presents by itself.

From the very start, then, we must clarify the meaning of the Bible's basic claim to be "the word of God." We must understand that this claim does not mean that the Bible is an entirely unworldly book, a message from eternity, a contemptuous dismissal of the world in a promulgation issued from "out there" beyond the confines of time and space. The Bible is not a denial of the world, a rejection of man, a negation of time and history and a condemnation of all that has been done by man in his world and in history. Nor is the Bible something that is meant to be *superimposed* upon the world, man and history from the outside, an *added* revelation of a hidden extra meaning, something entirely beyond man's everyday concerns and his ordinary existence, something that has to be accepted even though superfluous, and given preference over the ordinary familiar reality which seems to us more relevant.

In other words, the basic claim of the Bible is not to be interpreted in such terms as these: "Yes, there is an ordinary world in which you live your normal life with your fellow men. But this world is wicked and you are insignificant. While continuing to live in it and to obey its rules, you have to carefully learn a whole new body of truths which will seem to you senseless and incomprehensible, and you must add this superstructure of strange ideas on to what you see and know by your natural reason. You must now live in two worlds at the same time, one visible and the other invisible; one comprehensible and the other incomprehensible; one familiar and the other frightening and strange; one where you can be yourself and another where you must strive to be unnaturally 'good'; one which you instinctively take to be real, but which you must repudiate for the other which is truly real, though to you it seems totally superfluous."

This divisive and destructive pattern of life and thought is not the Bible message at all. The message of the Bible is precisely a message of unity and reconciliation, an all-embracing and positive revelation from which nothing real is excluded and in which all receives its full due and its ultimate meaning. One-sided distortions of the Bible have made it seem partial, and have restricted it to narrow, exclusive areas of "the sacred" and "the devout," as if to understand God's message one had to shut out God's world and man and history and time. As if faith meant the formal acceptance of the irrational and the absurd. As if one had to live by reason and common sense while at the same time repudiating and ridiculing them.

When viewed in this way the Bible becomes a kind of enormous cinder lodged in the eye of the world, blocking all normal vision and substituting pain, darkness and tears for the joy of daylight. In saying that we must expect to be outraged by the Bible, I am not trying to maintain that we must let it insult our intelligence. The Bible may be difficult and confusing, but it is meant to challenge our intelligence, not insult it. It becomes insulting when it is distorted by fanaticism and by foolish religiosity; but we must not blame the Bible for the distortions imposed on it by others.

Nevertheless, and quite apart from the question of theological faith (which is a special problem in itself), modern man may find himself wondering, in all honesty, whether the Bible is even *readable*. So much of it is archaic. So much is seemingly exotic, utterly alien to life as we know it now. True, our own civilization is still full of resonances from Judeo-Christian culture, therefore from the Bible. True, that in "searching the Scriptures" we may find, if not Christ as a living reality, at least some echoes of familiar ideas. But should we read the Bible merely for the comfort of discovering the source of a few religious clichés?

Perhaps many modern readers of the Bible will never get around to the classic questions and challenges of faith. Before one can seriously ask about theological belief, one may have to struggle with a more human question: "Must I believe that this is a good book? Must I believe that this is great literature? Must I claim that this book interests me more than my favorite magazine? Can I honestly affirm that I get more spontaneously involved in the Bible than I do in TV commercials?" Once again, this may be made more difficult by the superstition that the Bible has nothing to do with ordinary life and that it is enshrined in a special, sacred sphere, that in reading it one is somehow lifted out of time and space and transported to "eternity."

In order to read the Bible honestly, we have to avoid entrenching ourselves behind official positions, whether religious or cultural, whether for or against the Bible itself. The book is surrounded by every possible kind of myth and superstition, whether religious or anti-religious, theistic or atheistic, scientific or anti-scientific. The modern reader is plunged into a field of conscious and unconscious tensions even before he opens the book. He has to take this into account, too, and try to live with it. It is nothing new, and it is not even peculiar to modern man. It was known even in the so-called ages of faith when the Bible was set up, not against Marx, Freud and Nietzsche, but against Homer, Virgil and Sophocles.

Jerome, the fourth-century monk and translator of the Bible into Latin (the Vulgate), faced this problem in his own peculiarly ambivalent way. He knew that the Greek and Latin classics were in fact better than the Bible merely as "literature," and that there were far different reasons for reading the Bible. Yet nevertheless the literary quality of the Bible is something quite peculiar, because the literary experience of the authors (hence too of the understanding reader) is more than literary. It is religious, sometimes even to the point of being "prophetic" or "mystical" or "eschatological." Yet the prophetic and eschatological qualities of the experience are grounded in history and ordinary life.

In other words, even to appreciate much of the Bible as literature one has to come to terms with the fact that it gives literary expression to an experience that is more than aesthetic. Not only is it beyond literature, it is also in a certain sense beyond "religion"—beyond the devout and cleansing awe of initiation into ritual and mystery, beyond the healing and transforming sense of moral self-transcendence.

The Bible claims to contain a message which will not merely instruct you, not merely inform you about the distant past, not merely teach you certain ethical principles, or map out a satisfying hypothesis to explain your place in the universe and give your life meaning—much more than that, the Bible claims to be: The Word of God.

But what is this "word of God"? Is it simply a word of supreme and incontestable authority? Does it impose on man an outrageous doctrine which has no real meaning for his life, but which has to be accepted under penalty of going to hell? Once again, this utter distortion of the Bible is the result of fragmentation, division, and partiality. The prophets themselves protested, in God's name, against the perversion of the word of God in the interests of sectarianism, nationalism, power, politics. (See Jeremiah 23:23-40). To set up some limited human interest as an absolute to be blindly believed, followed and obeyed even unto death is to set up a "dead word," a destructive and idolatrous word in the place of the "living word" of God. "For the word of God is living and active, sharper than any two-edged sword, piercing to the division of soul and spirit, of joints and marrow, and discerning the thoughts and intentions of the heart" (Hebrews 4:12).

The basic claim made by the Bible for the word of God is not so much that it is to be blindly accepted because of God's authority, but that *it is recognized by its transforming and liberating power*. The "word of God" is recognized in actual experience because it does something to anyone who really "hears" it: it transforms his entire existence. Thus Paul writes to the Thessalonians: "And we also thank God constantly for this, that when you received the word of God which you heard from us, you accepted it not as the word of men but as what it really is, the word of God, which is at work in your believers" (1 Thessalo-

nians 2:13). But this "operation" of the word of
God penetrating our inmost being is more than
a communication of light: it is a new birth, the
beginning of a new being:

> Now there was a man of the Pharisees,
> named Nicodemus, a ruler of the Jews. This
> man came to Jesus by night and said to him,
> "Rabbi, we know that you are a teacher
> come from God; for no one can do these
> signs that you do, unless God is with him."
> Jesus answered him, "Truly, truly, I say to
> you, unless one is born anew, he cannot see
> the kingdom of God." Nicodemus said to
> him, "How can a man be born when he is
> old? Can he enter a second time into his
> mother's womb and be born?" Jesus an-
> swered, "Truly, truly, I say to you, unless
> one is born of water and the Spirit, he can-
> not enter the kingdom of God. That which
> is born of the flesh is flesh, and that which
> is born of the Spirit is spirit. Do not marvel
> that I said to you, 'You must be born anew.'
> The wind blows where it wills, and you hear
> the sound of it, but you do not know whence
> it comes or whither it goes; so it is with
> every one who is born of the Spirit." Nico-
> demus said to him, "How can this be?" Jesus
> answered him, "Are you a teacher of Israel,
> and yet you do not understand this?" (John
> 3:1-10).

Here again there is an implicit contrast between
the dry, academic and official learning *about* reli-

gion and the living power of the word. Paul too contrasts the deadening study of the "letter" with the living power of the spirit which is the true communication by which God manifests himself not in information but in life-giving power: thus in writing to the Corinthians, Paul wants them to understand that his communication of the message of God to them is not a matter of ink and paper but of the new life that has sprung up within them:

> You yourselves are our letter of recommendation, written on your hearts, to be known and read by all men; and you show that you are a letter from Christ delivered by us, written not with ink but with the Spirit of the living God, not on tablets of stone but on tablets of human hearts. Such is the confidence that we have through Christ toward God. Not that we are sufficient of ourselves to claim anything as coming from us; our sufficiency is from God, who has qualified us to be ministers of a new covenant, not in a written code but in the Spirit; for the written code kills, but the Spirit gives life (2 Corinthians 3:2-6).

What is said here about "spirit" has more than a vague and sentimental reference. It must be understood in the light of the much more concrete theological statements about the power of the Spirit and of Love, the Spirit of Truth by whom the world was created, by whom Christ was raised from the dead, by whom and in whom all is to be consummated. This Spirit of liberty is ultimately a Spirit of love which makes us live not for ourselves but for one another: "For you were called to freedom, brethren; only do not use your freedom as an opportunity for the flesh, but through love be servants of one another. For the whole law is fulfilled in one word, 'You shall love your neighbor as yourself'" (Galatians 5:13-14).

One who is reborn in the Spirit and who therefore lives by love is liberated from all the narrow claims of sectarian prejudice, nationalism, legalism, and from every division that breeds hatred and conflict. "But if you are led by the Spirit you are not under the law. Now the works of the flesh are plain: immorality, impurity, licentiousness, idolatry, sorcery, enmity, strife, jealousy, anger, selfishness, dissension, party spirit, envy, drunkenness, carousing, and the like. I warn you, as I warned you before, that those who do such things shall not inherit the kingdom of God" (Galatians 5:18-21). The word of God is then able to prove itself by its transforming power which brings love, unity, peace, understanding and freedom where before there were prejudice, conflict, hatred, division and greed.

The message of the Bible is then that into the confusion of man's world, with its divisions and hatred, has come a message of transforming power, and those who believe it will experience in themselves the love that makes for reconciliation and peace on earth.

> "If a man loves me, he will keep my word, and my Father will love him, and we will come to him and make our home with him. He who does not love me does not keep my words; and the word which you hear is not mine but the Father's who sent me. These things I have spoken to you, while I am still with you. But the Counselor, the Holy Spirit, whom the Father will send in my name, he will teach you all things, and bring to your remembrance all that I have said to you. Peace I leave with you; my peace I give to you; not as the world gives do I give to you. Let not your hearts be troubled, neither let them be afraid" (John 14:23-27).

If this power appears to have failed and not to have shown its full efficacy, perhaps it is the believers who have failed the Bible and not the other way around. In any case, the Bible itself takes account of this possible failure; that too is part of the message:

> "I have come as light into the world that whoever believes in me may not remain in darkness. If any one hears my sayings and does not keep them, I do not judge him; for I did not come to judge the world but to save the world. He who rejects me and does not receive my sayings has a judge; the word that I have spoken will be his judge on the

last day. For I have not spoken on my own authority; the Father who sent me has himself given me commandment what to say and what to speak. And I know that his commandment is eternal life. What I say, therefore, I say as the Father has bidden me" (John 12:46-50).

This idea of the power of the "word of God" is something that is clearly implicit in most of the books of the Bible, so that when you read the Bible, irrespective of whether you believe, you are reading a book in which, according to the authors, it is God rather than man who speaks to you. This is, of course, more true of some books than of others, but at any rate many of the authors not only believed they were "sent" as messengers of God but even resisted and tried to evade such a dangerous task before they finally took it on:

And I said: "Woe is me! For I am lost; for I am a man of unclean lips, and I dwell in the midst of a people of unclean lips; for my eyes have seen the King, the Lord of hosts!" Then flew one of the seraphim to me, having in his hand a burning coal which he had taken with tongs from the altar. And he touched my mouth and said: "Behold, this has touched your lips; your guilt is taken away, and your sin forgiven." And I heard the voice of the Lord saying, "Whom shall I send, and who will go for us?" Then I said, "Here I am! Send me." And he said, "Go, and say to this people: 'Hear and hear, but do not understand; see and see, but do not perceive.' Make the heart of this people fat, and their ears heavy, and shut their eyes; lest they see with their eyes, and hear with their ears, and understand with their hearts, and turn and be healed." Then I said, "How long, O Lord?" And he said: "Until cities lie waste without inhabitant, and houses without men, and the land is utterly desolate..." (Isaiah 6:5-11).

Now the word of the Lord came to me saying, "Before I formed you in the womb I knew you, and before you were born I consecrated you; I appointed you a prophet to the nations." Then I said, "Ah, Lord God! Behold, I do not know how to speak, for I am only a youth." But the Lord said to me, "Do not say, 'I am only a youth'; for to all to whom I send you you shall go, and whatever I command you you shall speak. Be not afraid of them, for I am with you to deliver you, says the Lord." Then the Lord put forth his hand and touched my mouth; and the Lord said to me, "Behold, I have put my words in your mouth. See, I have set you this day over nations and over kingdoms, to pluck up and to break down, to destroy and to overthrow, to build and to plant" (Jeremiah 1:4-10).

But Moses said to the Lord, "Oh, my Lord, I am not eloquent, either heretofore or since thou hast spoken to thy servant; but I am slow of speech and of tongue." Then the Lord said to him, "Who has made man's mouth? Who makes him dumb, or deaf, or seeing or blind? Is it not I, the Lord? Now therefore go, and I will be with your mouth and teach you what you shall speak" (Exodus 4:10-12).

Quite apart from the technical problem of interpretation of these passages, it is obvious that they are somehow claiming that there has been a breakthrough of the ultimate word into the sphere of the human, and that what the Bible is about is this breakthrough, recorded in events, happenings, which are decisive not only for the Jewish people or for the disciples of Christ but for mankind as a whole.

The Bible, then, claims to record these happenings, these breakthroughs, these invasions of man's private and complex world, by an ultimate Freedom which is at once the ground and source of man's being, the center of his history and the guide of his destinies. The mysterious word for that freedom is a non-word—for we know that in late Old Testament times the Name of God remained unspoken, unwritten, and eventually almost entirely unknown. The Jews remembered that he had a Name and had revealed it, but no one knew precisely what had been revealed. The letters YHWH were simply a *substitute for* the real Name that was unspoken and all-holy. Other terms—Elohim, Adonai, Lord, God, etc.—are all likewise substitutes for names and words which we do not possess.

The word "God," then, is in reality a non-word; yet behind it is a presence which fills the whole Bible like the smoke that filled Solomon's temple or the pillar of fire and cloud over the tabernacle. *Who is this?* Never does the Bible clearly explain. You are supposed to know. How? Another problem. The claims of the Bible are implicitly based, in part, on certain things that are taken for granted: for instance, some such fundamental intuition as that of our own identity, an intuition which is inseparably involved in an obscure awareness of ultimate identity. From the moment there is any "Who" at all, anyone to hear at all, there is the implication of an identity aware of itself. The ground of this awareness, what is it? Or *who* is it?

The curiously oblique yet insistent claims that underlie the very words of the Bible, quite apart from any interpretation of Church or Synagogue, quite apart from their employment in preaching and message, raise the fundamental question of *identity*. It may be too much to suggest that underlying the Bible is a powerful metaphysic of identity. Or should we go further? Does the Bible contain a theological revelation of identity beyond all grasp of metaphysics? *In any case the Bible raises the question of identity in a way no other book does*. As Barth pointed out: when you begin to question the Bible you find that the Bible is also questioning you. When you ask: "What is this book?" you find that you are also implicitly being asked: "Who is this that reads it?"

Is such a view alien to modern experience? Perhaps at first sight it may seem so. And one must not give the impression of claiming, as some popular preachers do, that you cannot seriously open the Bible without being instantly subject to various supernatural jolts, shocks, short circuits, mystical feedback, and heaven knows what else besides. Much more common reactions are boredom, mystification, a sense that one has suddenly got lost, and even the onset of sleep.

Everyone is likely to have trouble with the Bible, even the believer—perhaps *especially* the believer. The fact of unconscious revolt against the Bible on the part of ministers and priests whose lives are committed to its message is something that has a profound effect in religion. This has never been seriously studied. It would probably help account for much that is disconcerting and perverse—much that is rigid, callous, inhuman, fanatical—in the religious sphere. Someone like Dietrich Bonhoeffer can frankly admit his difficulty, and he did so even when he was facing death in prison. Such admissions are healthy. They clear the air a little for the rest of us.

> I am going through another spell of finding it difficult to read the Bible. I never know quite what to make of it. I don't feel guilty at all about it and I know it won't be long before I return to it again with renewed zest. Is it just a psychological process? I am almost inclined to think so... True, there is always a danger of indolence, but it would be wrong to get fussed about it. Far better to trust that after wobbling a bit the compass will come to rest in the right direction (*Prison Letters*).

This unusual capacity of a serious believer to accept without guilt a temporary repugnance for the Bible is in fact very revealing.

The truth is that the surface of the Bible is not always even interesting. And yet when one does finally get into it, in one way or other, when one at last catches on to the Bible's peculiar way of saying things, and even more to the things that are said, one finds that he is no longer simply questioning the book but being questioned by it.

This is, of course, common to all profound experience, not only in Christianity and Judaism but in all religion that gets beyond the level of superstition. All religion is concerned with man in the deepest roots of his own truth, of his own identity. Even when such language is invalidated and rejected completely, the thing it tries to signify remains—perhaps as a totally inarticulate, impenetrable, even painful fact. It is something that, however you look at it, is "given" to man along with his existence. He may try to forget it or try to ignore it, but the fact is that he is somebody—but *who?* And how does one find out?

Many religious books have approached this question in many different ways. In Zen Buddhism, which is definitely *not* a religion of books, there is a *mondo*, a kind of basic existential question, that springs out of a dialog between master and disciple and which remains for the disciple to solve by personal struggle. It goes like this: the disciple goes to his Master and asks: "Who is the Buddha?" The Master replies: "Who are *you?*"

The fact is that a question of this sort is, and must be, fundamental to all authentic religious experience—as well as to any radical metaphysical intuition and to mystical contemplation. In the first place it is itself an answer to a question. In the progress toward religious understanding, one does not go from answer to answer but from question to question. One's questions are answered, not by clear, definitive answers, but by more pertinent and more crucial questions. In the case of the Zen master and his disciple, the disciple asks a general, abstract, doctrinal question—one which could admit of any amount of theoretical elaboration. The Master replies with a direct, existential, concrete question to which there is no theoretical answer, and which no amount of verbalizing will be able to penetrate. It has to be grappled with in an entirely different way.

The same is true of the Bible. If we approach it with speculative questions, we are apt to find that it confronts us in turn with brutally practical questions. If we ask it for information about the meaning of life, it answers by asking us when we intend to start living? Not that it demands that we present suitable credentials, that we prove ourselves in earnest, but more than that: we are to understand life not by analyzing it but by living it in such a way that we come to a full realization of our own identity. And this of course means a full realization of our relatedness to those with whom life has brought us into an intimate and personal encounter.

Ultimately this means (in some way or other) a self-realization in the presence of an absolute Freedom who at once denies and affirms us; who is at once the ground of our freedom and its adversary; who accepts us in proportion as we renounce ourselves and who affirms us in so far as we live at the center of our existence rather than at its periphery. An ultimate Free-one who affirms us in so far as we are identified with him.

> Then Jesus told his disciples, "If any man would come after me, let him deny himself and take up his cross and follow me. For whoever would save his life will lose it, and whoever loses his life for my sake will find it. For what will it profit a man, if he gains the whole world and forfeits his life? Or what shall a man give in return for his life? (Matthew 16:24-26).

> For God sent the Son into the world, not to condemn the world, but that the world might be saved through him. He who believes in him is not condemned; he who does not believe is condemned already, because he has not believed in the name of the only Son of God. And this is the judgment, that the light has come into the world, and men loved darkness rather than light, because their deeds were evil. For everyone who does evil hates the light, and does not come to the light, lest his deeds should be exposed. But he who does what is true comes to the light, that it may be clearly seen that his deeds have been wrought in God (John 3:17-21).

> Truly, truly, I say to you, unless a grain of wheat falls into the earth and dies, it remains alone; but if it dies, it bears much fruit. He

who loves his life loses it, and he who hates his life in this world will keep it for eternal life. If any one serves me, he must follow me; and where I am, there shall my servant be also; if any one serves me, the Father will honor him (John 12:24-26).

One of the central points of Johannine theology is that Christ is in that ultimate center, speaks out of that center, that it speaks in and through him so that a personal commitment to the truth and love manifested in the preaching of Christ means "remaining in him" (John 15:5) and hence in the ultimate and absolute center of all understanding and all freedom:

And Jesus cried out and said, "He who believes in me, believes not in me but in him who sent me. And he who sees me sees him who sent me. I have come as light into the world that whoever believes in me may not remain in darkness. If anyone hears my sayings and does not keep them, I do not judge him; for I did not come to judge the world but to save the world. He who rejects me and does not receive my sayings has a judge; the word that I have spoken will be his judge on the last day. For I have not spoken on my own authority; the Father who sent me has himself given me commandment what to say and what to speak. And I know that his commandment is eternal life. What I say, therefore, I say as the Father has bidden me" (John 12:44-50).

Thus if we ask the Bible, as we ultimately must when we enter into serious dialog with it: "Who is this Father? What is meant by Father? Show us the Father?" we in our turn are asked in effect: "Who are *you* who seek to know 'the Father' and what do you think you are seeking anyway?" And we are told: Find yourself in love of your brother as if he were Christ (since in fact he 'is Christ') and you will know the Father (see John 14:8-17). That is to say: if you live *for others* you will have an intimate personal knowledge of the love that rises up in you out of a ground that lies beyond your own freedom and your own inclination, and yet is present as the very core of your own free and personal identity. Penetrating to that inner ground of love you at last find your true self.

This is not the place to develop basic themes in New Testament theology, but examples are necessary precisely because the claims of the Bible are theological. The question of identity and of meaning is raised not merely in psychological and ethical terms, not merely in dogmatic and revealed mysteries, but in terms of theological self-commitment, that is to say, of a faith which goes beyond mere assent to dogmatic propositions and becomes a personal encounter with the unknown for whom there is a non-word, "God," and also a more concrete, humanly biased name, "Father." (Remember that somehow Christ immediately cancels the word "Father" in the word "Son"—for the two are identical, and later theology understood the immense importance of this identity; it is the ultimate root of all human freedom.)

So, as Karl Barth so well said: "The question we ask becomes a question asked of us, in face of which we are thrown into a strangely embarrassing position between 'Yes' and 'No' (*Word of God and Word of Man*, Torchbook ed., p. 53).

Barth also makes plain that this kind of confrontation is not inevitable. There are many less radical ways of reading the Bible. Curiously, the most serious religious people, or the most concerned scholars, those who constantly read the Bible as a matter of professional or pious duty, can often manage to evade a radically involved dialogue with the book they are questioning. In fact (we know it too well!) there is such a thing as studying the isolated words and other details with such intense application that one loses all interest in their meaning.

We are fortunately living in an age of theological ferment and of Biblical renewal. All of us—

scholars, simple believers or mere interested readers—stand in immense debt to the specialists who
have done so much to really open the Bible to us.
Nevertheless, in all the thousands of pages of
Biblical scholarship that have been printed in the
last hundred years we must admit, and anyone
well read in the field must agree, that a high proportion of it is an arid, exhausting desert of futile
detail which wearies the mind by distracting it
from the meaning of the Bible and goes wandering
aimlessly through a wilderness of technicalities
where all interest withers and expires.

Good Biblical scholarship is essential for a
serious understanding of the Bible, but this scientific itch for arid and pointless investigations which
throw no new light on anything whatever has
deadened our sensitivity to the existential reality
of Biblical experience. Doubtless that is what
Barth means when he says: "The Bible gives to
every man and to every era such answers to their
questions as they deserve. We shall always find
in it as much as we seek and no more . . . nothing
whatever if it is nothing whatever that we seek."

This is of course very true, and yet one must
qualify it by experience; for the relationship between the reader and the word is a dynamic one
—"living and efficacious"—and in that relationship much more happens than we expect and much
more is found that we originally started out to
seek.

And so, Barth continues, "we must trust ourselves to reach eagerly for an answer which is
really much too large for us, for which we are
really not ready, and of which we do not seem
worthy, since it is a fruit which our own longing,
striving and inner labor have not planted" (*Word
of God and Word of Man*, p. 32).

Surprisingly, this ability to reach far beyond
ourselves and to find what we never expected in
the Bible is by no means a special privilege of the
biblical expert or even of the pious believer. On
the contrary, we have to recognize that those for
whom the Bible has become a habit may well
defraud themselves of deeper understanding by
deciding in advance what they want of the Bible
and what it wants of them. They go to the Bible
knowing in just what ways it suits them. They
dig into it to satisfy their own needs—and of
course they are not wrong. But the Bible is not
there merely to satisfy our needs or to give us
what suits us.

On the contrary, the Biblical message may
seem at first sight to be something that does not
suit us at all in any way, culturally, ethically,
spiritually, theologically. It may be supremely disconcerting, ambiguous, even frightening. It may
shock our reason into unbelief, and we may have
to struggle with it as a scandal. Indeed, when
closely examined, the Bible may pose a threat to
what has hitherto seemed to us to be "faith."

There is, in a word, nothing comfortable about the Bible—until we manage to get so used to it that we make it comfortable for ourselves. But then we are perhaps too used to it and too at home in it. Let us not be too sure we know the Bible just because we have learned not to be astonished at it, just because we have learned not to have problems with it. Have we perhaps learned at the same time not to really pay attention to it? Have we ceased to question the book and be questioned by it? Have we ceased to fight it? Then perhaps our reading is no longer serious.

For most people, the understanding of the Bible is, and should be, a struggle: not merely to find meanings that can be looked up in books of reference, but to come to terms personally with the stark scandal and contradiction in the Bible itself. It should not be our aim merely to explain these contradictions away, but rather to use them as ways to enter into the strange and paradoxical world of meanings and experiences that are beyond us and yet often extremely and mysteriously relevant to us.

Those who do not believe, and who think themselves impervious to the supposed irrationality of belief, are sometimes in a better position to enter into dialog and struggle with the Bible than believers themselves. To begin with, once they work up enough interest in the book to take it seriously, they are not afraid to fight it. They are not held back by guilt feelings. They do not hesitate to admit that they find the sacred book ambiguous. They make no bones about doubting that it is "the word of God." Reading it as the word of man and that only, they may proceed more freely and more intelligently than the believer who is so intent on good and reverent manners that he perhaps unconsciously closes himself to the book by his very devotion—as if he were afraid to find in it something incredible.

It follows that the believer should not cling too complacently to his status and apparent privilege, as if the Bible were *his* book exclusively and as if *he* knew all about it. On the contrary, the ecumenical perspectives of our time have taught us to regret the madness of our fathers, who tended to go to war with each other over detailed questions of biblical interpretation, each one believing that he and his community alone were right and chosen.

Now we are beginning to see even further than that: the Bible is everybody's book, and the unbeliever can prove himself as capable as anyone else of finding new aspects of it which the believer would do well to take seriously.

Take, for example, the case of the Italian Marxist Pasolini and his extraordinary response to the Gospel of St. Matthew. The story is rather well known: John XXIII was visiting Assisi—something quite new for a twentieth-century Pope, who should, everyone thought, have remained walled up in the Vatican where he belonged. But Pope John was loose, and he had all the traffic in Assisi snarled up; one could not even go out into the street for hours. Everything was packed solid with people.

So while the "prisoner of the Vatican" was disrupting the secular life of Assisi, the Marxist had to remain a prisoner in his hotel room. He happened to find a Bible there, and to pass the time he picked it up and read the Gospel of St. Matthew. The film that resulted was dedicated to the memory of John XXIII.

The value of the film lay in its extraordinary sincerity and authenticity. To begin with, it was obviously made on a very small budget indeed —somewhere out in the rocks of a very poor part of Italy. The cast were not professional actors but just "people"—most of them poor and some of them Communists. Pasolini himself played St. Peter, and his mother the Virgin Mary. The result was a kind of cinematic passion play, with a visual authenticity approaching the Florentine or Sienese painting of the 15th century (though without color). The contrast with the vulgar and lavish artificiality of Hollywood was, to say the least, impressive.

Many Christians who saw the film criticized it, not because it was unfaithful to the Gospel, but because it presented a picture of Christ that frightened them. The Christ of Pasolini, young, dark, splendidly aloof, dreadfully serious, was obviously not the sweet, indulgent Jesus of late nineteenth-century Church art. And the apostles were obviously not unreal, shadowy ghosts incapable of understanding a single fact about human existence. These were very real, gnarled, tough men, weather-beaten people who had lived through cruel wars, who had hidden in the mountains from the political police, who knew what the inside of prisons and concentration camps looked like—in a word, they resembled the actual men Christ chose for his disciples!

The Christ of Pasolini was not indulgent, he was demanding. He was not soft, he was unyielding. On certain points one felt he could be almost merciless. The fact that so many Christians could be shocked by this is itself shocking, for this picture of Christ obviously rested on a very real and open-minded reading of St. Matthew! The only Gospel that is tougher is perhaps Mark's. Have we forgotten that love can be demanding, exacting, unyielding? Especially when it encounters indifference to the sufferings of others and a disposition to cheat and exploit them without mercy? The Christ of St. Matthew can rigorously demand that men have mercy on one another as the only way to make them ready to receive mercy (cf. Matthew 5:7; 21:31-46).

The film was, therefore, a very plausible and convincing interpretation of the Gospel. This interpretation was possible precisely because the director and the actors had all personally *discovered* the Gospel of Matthew in making the film. They could not have attained such a refreshing success if they had been used to, perhaps tired of, a routine and trifling exposure to the Bible. It was new to them, and in their reading of Matthew, their interpretation of it, they had to take up a definite position in regard to its message. They responded to the Bible in a way that also implied a definite position toward the world of their own time. They made a certain connection between the modern world and the message of Christ. They took a definite stand in regard to who Christ was, at least according to the report of this Gospel. Furthermore, in making a film of such seriousness, they obviously decided that this report was at least in one sense *highly credible*. They endowed it with the quality of credibility which was perhaps all the more impressive because it tended to by-pass theology and accept Christ and the disciples in all their human reality

—as portrayed in the eminently human literary work which is the Gospel of Matthew.

Theology cannot afford to be insensitive to such things, and when it becomes too abstract, when it empties Christ and the Gospel of this flesh-and-blood reality which the Gospel writers themselves put into it so convincingly, it certainly does not help us to be better believers in Christ as Son of God. Whatever one may decide about the Christian message of the Incarnation, there is nothing to gain theologically by treating Christ as if he were not the "Son of Man"—the title by which he habitually refers to himself in Matthew.

In the end, no matter what one might ultimately think of Marxism and of the possible implications of Pasolini's view of Christ, this film was a very respectable and serious response to the Bible. This was made possible by a serious decision of Pasolini to find Christ, his apostles and his message entirely credible, at least in human and artistic terms. In so doing, he necessarily ended by making a powerful statement about Christ, man and the world. The cast and their director were enabled to do this by the fact that they became involved in the Gospel, acting out this story, and identifying themselves personally with the apostles. The statement in its turn is valuable for believers, enabling them to recover some of the sense of urgency, freshness and renewal which is essential if we are to continue

with the same kind of self-discovery. For it was
evident that the men who went through the experience of making such a movie arrived at a new
self-discovery by identifying themselves with the
disciples of the Son of Man.

☆   ☆   ☆

In other words, any serious reading of the
Bible means personal involvement in it, not simply
mental agreement with abstract propositions. And
involvement is dangerous, because it lays one
open to unforeseen conclusions. That is why we
prefer if possible to remain uninvolved. In 2
Samuel 12:1-10, we read how David, a man of
quick and hot emotional response, listens to a
story of Nathan and becomes involved in it to
the point of intense and righteous indignation,
and then discovers that the malefactor who so
angers him is *himself!*

We all instinctively know that it is dangerous
to become involved in the Bible. The book judges
us, or seems to judge us, on terms to which at
first we could not possibly agree.

The Bible itself, in the Book of Job, gives us
a pattern of healthy *disagreement*. Not only that,

but throughout the whole Old Testament in particular we find people (like Abraham) arguing with God and being implicitly praised for it. The point is, then, that becoming involved in the Bible does not mean simply taking everything it says without the slightest murmur of difficulty. It means at once being willing to argue and fight back, provided that if we are clearly wrong we will finally admit it. The Bible prefers honest disagreement to a dishonest submission.

One of the basic truths put forward in the Bible as a whole is not merely that God is always right and man is always wrong, but that God and man can face each other in an authentic dialog: one which implies *a true reciprocity between persons, each of whom fully respects the other's rights and his freedom.* The covenant idea, as Erich Fromm rightly observed, brings this out clearly. And we should remark in passing that the so-called "anthropomorphic" portrayal of God in human form—so often complained of by people who believe the Bible is not sufficiently "spiritual" —has this particular purpose. The whole idea of covenant, dialog, reciprocity, mutual respect—and above all the idea that God respects man's liberty, dignity, and rights—is brought out by giving the exchange a frankly human character. "Then the Lord said to Moses.... Then Moses replied." To complain of this is not to give evidence of superior mystical wisdom, but only of literal-mindedness and weak imagination.

nother example of a modern reading of the Bible outside the framework of official belief is that of a man we mentioned a moment ago, the psychoanalyst Erich Fromm. Dr. Fromm belongs to that category of men, surely large in the world today, who are neither believers nor unbelievers, neither theists nor atheists. Like Camus, Fromm makes clear that he is "not a theist." This carefully chosen expression implies also that he is not a (militant and "believing") atheist. But of course Fromm's position is a bit ambiguous because, as he does not hesitate to admit, he studied the Bible and the Talmud in childhood and received a Jewish formation.

Like Pasolini, but in an entirely different way, Fromm has searched the Bible for a certain fundamental and ultimate human relevance. He explains his approach in words which will surely be valid for many readers of the Bible who are unable to accept it as "divine revelation." They may well agree with Fromm that:

It is an extraordinary book, expressing many norms and principles that have maintained their validity throughout thousands of years. It is a book that has proclaimed a vision for men that is still valid and awaiting realization (*You Shall Be As Gods*, p. 7).

What is this vision? For Fromm it is a "radical humanism" which emphasizes *the oneness of the human race*, "the capacity of man to develop his own powers, and to arrive at inner harmony and at the establishment of a peaceful world." Certainly this is an authentic grasp of at least one of the most important aspects of the Bible, whether in the Old Testament or in the New.

The word which Isaiah the son of Amoz saw concerning Judah and Jerusalem. It shall come to pass in the latter days that the mountain of the house of the Lord shall be established as the highest of the mountains, and shall be raised above the hills; and all the nations shall flow to it, and many peoples shall come and say: "Come, let us go up to the mountain of the Lord, to the house of the God of Jacob; that he may teach us his ways and that we may walk in his paths." For out of Zion shall go forth the law, and the word of the Lord from Jerusalem. He shall judge between the nations, and shall decide for many peoples; and they shall beat their swords into plowshares, and their spears into pruning hooks; nation shall not lift up sword against nation, neither shall they learn war any more (Isaiah 2:1-4).

"I do not pray for these only, but also for those who are to believe in me through their word, that they may all be one; even as thou, Father, art in me, and I in thee, that they also may be in us, so that the world may believe that thou hast sent me. The glory which thou hast given me I have given to them, that they may be one even as we are one, I in them and thou in me, that they may become perfectly one, so that the world may know that thou hast sent me and hast loved them even as thou hast loved me" (John 17:20-23).

Fromm goes on to stress the importance of freedom in the Bible. The radical humanism which he finds there "considers the goal of man to be that of complete independence, and this implies penetrating through fictions and illusions to a full awareness of reality. It implies furthermore a skeptical attitude toward the use of force, precisely because during the history of man it has been and still is force—creating fear—which has made man ready to take fiction for reality, illusions for truth." One might be tempted to question and discuss some of these points, but the fact remains that both in the Old Testament and in the New the central message is one of liberation, not only from the bondage of Egypt, not only from the corruption of ambitious kings, not only from exile in Babylon, but from everything that corrupts the heart of man and enslaves him to anything less than himself. Indeed, one of the most baffling and (with reason) outrageous claims of the Bible is that in the end God intends to free man even from death! Certainly, then, we must take seriously the words of Christ, "The truth shall make you free" (John 8:32), and of Paul, "Stand fast therefore and do not submit again to a yoke of slavery" (Galatians 5:1).

Fromm is certainly right in his intuition that the prohibition of idolatry is in fact one of the deepest roots of this Biblical doctrine of liberty, idolatry being in fact inseparable from servitude to human systems that exploit man's natural needs and appetites for their own ends, or seek to dominate him by brute force. Idolatry is, of course, a basic form of spiritual violence. This was clearly understood in the non-violent resistance of the Christian martyrs against the idolatrous claims of the Roman State.

Sometimes religious people complain that we live in an age of godless materialism in which the message of the Bible has become meaningless and is callously ignored by modern man. Dr. Fromm on the contrary (and here again the example of Pasolini's film gives him support) says:

> Perhaps we today can understand the Hebrew Bible better than any age before precisely because we live in a time of revolution in which man, in spite of many errors that lead him into new forms of dependence, is shaking himself free from all forms of social bondage.... Perhaps, paradoxically enough, one of the oldest books of Western culture can be understood best by those who are least fettered by tradition and most aware of the radical process of liberation going on at the present time (*op. cit.*, p. 7).

Bonhoeffer too has brought up the crucial question of religious language in the modern world and has rightly pointed out that the problem is not in religious language and concepts themselves but rather in the toneless and empty routine discourse used by religious people. Bonhoeffer confessed that when talking to religious people he was embarrassed to speak of God, and was "oppressed and ill at ease," or even "dried up completely" when they used religious jargon. Yet he could speak more freely of God to non-religious people: "quite openly and as if it were a matter of course." This is a curiously modern problem, and it reminds us once again that the Bible is now *everybody's* book. It does not belong exclusively to the churches or to the religious, and perhaps the outsider who questions it sincerely may be able to see in it something that the believer has missed. Bonhoeffer adds:

> I often ask myself why a "Christian instinct" frequently draws me more to the non-religious than to the religious—and that too without any intention of evangelizing them but rather . . . in "brotherhood."

It is certainly true that all through the Bible we find what we might call the groundwork of a theology of liberation and resistance, even in the historical situation of the Jews and of the first Christians. The "People of God" to whom the message of liberty is directed is, in fact, a small nation or a minority in exile, constantly called upon to resist the massive power of invaders and oppressors, but to do so in a special way: trusting not in alliances with the big political powers but in the hidden, seemingly hazardous, but really firm promises of God. It is precisely in the soil of oppression and in the call for spiritual resistance that God sows the seed of that Biblical humanism which Fromm is not wrong in calling "radical." The prophetic vision of a "united, peaceful mankind, of justice for the poor and helpless" blazed out in what is essentially a dark and tragic situation, the Jews' loss of their home and even of their Temple.

We must never overlook the fact that the message of the Bible is above all a message preached to the poor, the burdened, the oppressed, the underprivileged. There is no need to remind the reader how Marx capitalized on the fact. But Marx assumed that the Bible was essentially a deliberate fraud on the part of a ruling class to deceive the poor and make them accept their lot by means of a mystification. This is not the place to spell out apologetic arguments against the Marxian contention that religion is the "opium of the people," when in fact we are also aware that even the revolutionary eschatology of Marx himself can be shown to be largely based on a biblical pattern. For precisely one of the central messages of the Bible is that the ultimate meaning of man's existence on earth is to be found in history, and that the human race is moving toward a final accounting in which history itself will see that the injustice of oppressors will be punished and those they oppressed will receive their just reward.

The Bible also points out that man is to act as God's collaborator in setting up a definitive kingdom of justice and peace (see 1 Corinthians 3:9; Colossians 1:39; Philippians 4:13; Ephesians 1:15-23). No doubt there is a vast difference between the mystical view of history taken by Paul, who sees the power of the Spirit "driving" the redeemed to accomplish an historic destiny of uniting all mankind in peace and reconciliation (see Ephesians 1:9-13), and Marx's dialectic of class struggle and the withering away of the state. Yet Marxism is a product of a long tradition of thought deeply influenced by the Bible and by Judaeo-Christian messianism. The eschatological mystique of Marxism, with its awareness of an underlying plan in history and of a final purpose which man, in his freedom, can help to actualize, would hardly have been possible without the Biblical background of European civilization.

Let us now consult one more example of a modern work of art in which the experience of "hearing the word" is described. This time we turn to William Faulkner's novel, *The Sound and the Fury*. We have by now become wise enough to realize that a writer can be profoundly Biblical in his work without being a churchgoer or a conventional believer, and we are also aware of the fact that in our time it is often the isolated and lonely artist, facing the problems of life without the routine consolations of conventional religion, who really experiences in their depth the existential dimensions of those problems.

Faulkner was certainly one such artist, and we know that he even devoted several years to working out an explicitly religious and Christian allegory (in *A Fable*). This book, as it happened, was one of his failures. But in other novels in which he was perhaps less deliberate and less self-conscious in his effort, he succeeded in penetrating the heart of the Biblical message, though perhaps in obscure and highly paradoxical ways. The tragic ironies of a book like *Light in August* are stretched out to such an extreme that most people would not only hesitate to see it as a kind of perverse Christology, but would even be revolted by the thought. Yet that is the case, as I hope to show elsewhere.

In the last section of *The Sound and the Fury*, describing the Easter service at the little Negro church, Faulkner presents us with one of the most authentic and most moving accounts of a deep Biblical experience. This experience is precisely the authentic hearing of the message of God, the message of the Bible, preached and received with faith in a congregation of simple and sincere believers. Seldom has any American writer—or any writer at all—given us such a powerfully convincing insight into what it means to *hear the word* that has been given to mankind in the Bible.

At this point, even if only in passing, we must remember that the Bible (which we think of as a book to be *read*) was originally a body of oral traditions meant to be *recited and listened to in a group especially attuned to its message.* The Bible is not primarily a written or printed text to be scrutinized in private, in a scholar's study or a contemplative cell. It is a body of oral messages, announcements, prophecies, promulgations, recitals, histories, songs of praise, lamentations, etc., which are meant either to be uttered or at least read aloud, or chanted, or sung, or recited *in a community convoked for the purpose of a living celebration.* Such a convocation is a synagogue or church (*ekklesia*—community of those called to hear and respond).

Thus we should realize that the Biblical message is something that establishes and confirms a community, a convocation, in its identity. The common reaction of belief, response, acceptance, affirmation, praise and thanksgiving by which the "word" is not simply understood but *celebrated*, is essential to a full understanding of the Bible. In fact, the Jewish and Christian understanding of the Bible has never been the work merely of scholars and specialists; it has been the fruit of collective and communal celebration, and the transmission of a common *experience* of receiving the word of God from generation to generation. This, of course, is a complex, many-sided phenomenon, and in so far as it is a human, cultural phenomenon we may look for ambiguous and perhaps corrosive elements in it.

In his description of the Easter service in *The Sound and the Fury*, Faulkner made a classic statement not only on the American South, not only on the Negro, not only on the Church in its most authentic reality, but also on the entire meaning of human existence. And he made this statement in fundamentally Biblical terms.

We can compare the simplicity of the Negro cook Dilsey with the complexities of the other characters in other works where Faulkner attempts to work out the same kind of artistic solution. Dilsey stands out above all of them in a lucid clarity which is due entirely to the fact that she is Christian. She is the only fully and unambiguously Christian character in Faulkner (Nancy Mannigoe, in *Requiem for a Nun*, is not unambiguous!).

The household of Jason Compson (where Dilsey is employed as cook and housekeeper) verifies the title of the book. It is full of noise, fury, madness, passion, hatred, conflict and cruelty —the typical Faulkner recipe! But when the time comes for Dilsey to go to church with her relatives and the (white) idiot, Benjy Compson, we are shown a kind of solemn procession out of this violent world into a world of simplicity, poverty, honesty and biblical truth.

The solemn and simple processional bearing with which Dilsey leads her friends and relatives to worship has deeply Biblical resonances. At the very heart of the Bible is the theme of "passover" and exodus, the procession of the redeemed out of a doomed society into the desert, on the way to a promised kingdom. This becomes the *pascha Christi*, the exodus of Christ "out of this world to the Father" by death and resurrection. And of course the true meaning of Easter is precisely that the Christian is called to make this journey with Christ and the people of God out of "Egypt" to the promised land.

The Compson household is indeed a kind of Egypt of violent futility, and Jason, a Pharaoh straining every nerve to make others the slaves of his arbitrary will. The Negro church, depicted as a kind of large, amazing toy set precariously on the very edge of the world, is an eschatological symbol of the redeemed community. And those who "hear" the secret invitation gather together there spontaneously to form an *ekklesia*, to understand and celebrate the word of liberation. They are freed not only from fear and hell, but from unmeaning, hatred, confusion, the kingdom of Beelzebub symbolized by the obsessions of Jason Compson.

Yet not all is honest in the Negro church, where the visiting preacher from St. Louis begins by trying to imitate the rhetoric of an academic white pulpiteer. But when he suddenly sees "the recollection and the blood of the Lamb," the whole tone of the experience changes. The entire congregation responds to a sermon which, in its own crude and lovely poetry, condenses into a few moments the whole history of salvation—the whole Christian message about the meaning of life in love, redemption, reconciliation. And Dilsey, with tears streaming down her cheeks, with her face shining, has "seen the beginning and the end."

The sudden, extraordinary change of tempo and atmosphere, the transformation of Reverend Shegog from a religious careerist into a prophet of the word (as though by pentecostal intervention) is not merely a literary device to entertain the reader. It is again deeply Biblical, and perhaps more so than Faulkner himself could consciously realize. It suggests the deeper New Testament understanding of the liberation and exodus: the passage from external letter, which is dead, to life-giving Spirit, which cannot be held within the confines of mere decorous ritual observance. There is a Biblical breakthrough of the power of the word, flaming out in the midst of the fakery and tedious pomposity of conventional religion.

The corresponding transformation in Dilsey is completely Biblical. It is the fruit of an inner ripening which we have sensed in her all along. This is her *kairos*, her time of illumination and unburdening, her meeting with the creative and redemptive power of the Spirit which shows her all the world, all history and all the Bible gathered together in one flash, the "beginning and the end." To see this is to see the Christ of the Apocalypse, the Alpha and Omega, in whom everything is already fulfilled and of whose victory there can be no doubt.

That Dilsey attains this experience of *kairos* is due to the fact that her entire sense of time is Biblical from the start. The key to the understanding of *The Sound and the Fury* is the contrapuntal difference between the time-sense of the various characters. Benjy, the idiot, lives in a paradisal timelessness of pure nature. Here past, present and future merge in a symbiotic experience of a purely instinctual present. He is pre-religious in his sense of time, and also pre-civilized. Quentin Compson, obsessed by the ticking of clocks, who eventually commits suicide because time haunts him, and Jason, the business man, the reader of tickertapes and timetables, the sender of telegrams: both are types of civilized and rationalistic man, caught in the web of purely abstract time.

Dilsey has a time-sense that is entirely Biblical: not measured by the clock (the clock in her kitchen strikes five and she says "Hm, eight o'clock") but by the living fulness of organic growth. Her time is the time of life itself maturing in its own leisurely way. It is the time of love, which accepts the gradual pace of this maturing without trying to force matters and rejoices when the fruit is finally ripe. (Jason, of course, forces everything, time included.) Dilsey is then the one who is ready for the *kairos* because her whole sense of time is that which pervades the Bible itself. Only Dilsey knows time as fully and definitively "redeemed."

This is, of course, the real point of the Bible.

This dynamic of hearing, response, revelation, "unburdening" in the context of an event, a happening, is characteristic of the Bible, particularly *in the way it revolutionizes our experience of time*, making it concrete rather than abstract.

All the great religious classics in all traditions have certainly striven to give men the key to something, to an inner meaning, to a way of life, perhaps to a fundamental revolution of the personal or communal self-understanding, and all have reacted somehow to time and history (sometimes rejecting both as fundamental illusions).

Yet the Bible has a special character which sets it apart from all the others. Obviously, it is very important to know what this special character is, so that we may not expect the Bible to give us something that we might find more clearly expressed somewhere else.

When we say the Bible seeks to reveal to us the meaning of our existence, we must be careful to distinguish it from the metaphysical, or mystical, or ethical religious texts which describe or explain the basic constitution of reality itself and which build upon that description a formula for right living and perhaps for complete self-transcendence.

Obviously, scholars have brought out the intimate relationship between the Bible and other Oriental religious texts. We know, for instance, that the creation account in Genesis is couched in terms of myths that circulated all through the Near East. In this the Bible doubtless does have much in common with those ancient books which sought to express religious truth in mythical terms, and which (as scholars like Mircea Eliade have shown) were able to awaken deep resonances in the collective and personal unconscious, with its archetypal symbolic patterns, its dynamic of return to the origin, its affinity for centripetal, mandala-like patterns, its need for ritual enactment in order to intensify the religious consciousness.

Some archaic texts, like the *Vedas* of India, celebrate and praise the mythical gods in terms that express the deepest longing for immortality and eternal life long before the concept of an afterlife was clearly developed among the Jews. The *Upanishads* are perhaps the most profoundly contemplative collection of texts ever written, dealing with the metaphysical unity of Being and with the yogic consciousness of that unity in concentration and in self-transcending wisdom (*samadhi*).

The Taoist classics of China, the *Tao te ching* and the books attributed to Chuang Tzu, take a more direct, less speculative view of metaphysics and seek immediate apprehension of the ground of being not in mystical abstraction but in a full awareness of the transcendent dimensions of everyday life in its very ordinariness. This Chinese matter-of-factness joined with the teachings of Buddha (in themselves simpler and more concrete than Hindu speculation, though they were soon given an abstract philosophical form in India) and the result was Zen, a completely non-speculative and non-systematic way of direct vision into the ground of being.

In many ways Zen, which explicitly repudiates all authoritarian scriptures, is poles apart from the Bible, but in its uniquely zestful appreciation of the concrete happening and of concrete, living time, Zen does come close to the existentiality and spontaneity of the personal act of Biblical faith, though here we must distinguish carefully between faith in dogmatic propositions about God and faith as a personal, inscrutable *event and encounter* which revolutionizes one's entire sense of being and of identity.

The Confucian classics of China—on which the civilization of the Far East rested for nearly three millennia—placed great stress on the cultivation of moral and personal excellence: the formation of the "superior man" not simply by individual discipline, but above all by a sense of relatedness and of mutual obligation within the social community. The Bible does this too, and there is much in common between the Confucian ethic and that of the Wisdom literature in the Bible. This is not surprising because in fact this ethical wisdom, based on the demands and capacities of man in his basic humanity and in his native resources, was developed almost universally during the five centuries or so before Christ—the period which Karl Jaspers calls "axial"—during which man became conscious of personality, responsibility and freedom. No other ancient book gives such a deep and penetrating view of this development as does the Bible.

The Bible does not simply present us with another variation of ethical or metaphysical wisdom. It does not simply give us a particularly fortunate hypothesis to explain man and the universe and orient him toward a meaningful existence. The Bible does not only seek to explain

God, or tell us about his nature, his existence, his attributes, his inner life. The Bible does not seek to prove abstract propositions about God, though it is certainly concerned with affirming his reality in the most categorical and absolute fashion as against the falsity and mendacity of idols. But this affirmation of God's absolute being is itself mysterious, paradoxical, and seems to remain deliberately incomplete.

If the Bible does not pretend to give a satisfactory description or explanation of God, we must also recognize that it does not strive to give a scientific account of the physical universe in terms of God as first cause. It is true that the Bible does at times "account for" the world, but only in passing, in mythical and poetic terms which are obviously not translatable into some supposed scientific equivalent (as, for example, by taking the six days of creation as stages of evolutionary development). It is true that the Bible was assimilated into Greco-Roman and then European culture, and biblical thought became integrated with the science and philosophy of Greece and Rome.

But we must not confuse the Bible with the European civilization into which it was incorporated. If we do, then we run into difficulties, because we find a particular world-view in conflict with the modern, scientific world-view, and we assume that "God" is in fact embedded in an outworn scientific explanation of the world. He thus has no function other than that of accounting for what science does not understand. The more science understands, the more God is pushed into the background of remote, or intimate and personal problems.

As Bonhoeffer once observed, God is not simply a stop-gap for the holes in our knowledge of the world, nor is he merely the source of ultimate answers to personal and human problems. In other words, God is not simply the one whom we reach when we are extended to our own limits. He is, on the contrary, the ground and center of our existence, and though we may conceive ourselves as "going to" him and reaching out to him beyond the sphere of our everyday existence, we nevertheless start from him and remain in him as the very ground of our existence and reality.

He is not merely "out there" in a vague beyond. He is not merely hidden in the shadows of what is unknown, and pushed further and further away in proportion as we come to know more and more. He is the very ground of what we know, and our knowledge itself is his manifestation: not that he is the cause of all that is real, but that reality itself is his epiphany. The words of Bonhoeffer are profoundly biblical in their radical dismissal of "unworldly" faith that centers too exclusively on personal crisis and on the quest for an inner refuge from worldly conflict. It was not from the Bible that we learned to escape "into eternity," nor did the Bible teach us to seek peace in inwardness and defensive recollection. These are elements of another cultural and spiritual heritage. As Bonhoeffer says:

> We should find God in what we know, not in what we don't; not in outstanding problems but in those we have already solved.... We must not wait until we are at the end of our tether: he must be found at the center of life and not only in death; in health and vigor, and not only in suffering; in activity and not only in sin (*Prison Letters*, p. 191).

The Bible is a "worldly" book in this sense that it sees God at the very center of man's life, his work, his relations with his fellow man, his love of his wife and children, his play and his joy. On the contrary, it is characteristic of the idols that they are objectified and set up on the periphery of life. It is the idols who dominate specific areas of life from outside it, because they are in fact projections of man's fragmented desires and aspirations. It is the idols that man goes out to meet when he reaches his own limit, and they are called in to supplement his strength and his ingenuity when these run out. God is never shown by the Bible merely as a *supplement* of man's power and intelligence, but as its very ground and reality.

God is a definite presence and force in the Bible, and where necessary this real presence is made imaginable by the use of anthropomorphic language. There is also a definite progression from archaic concepts to a more sophisticated understanding.

The Bible is less concerned with great metaphysical problems (such as good and evil) than is a philosopher like Plato. The terrible "problem of suffering" is regarded by the Bible not so much as a problem to be explained or as a mystery to be contemplated, but as an inscrutable existential fact. The one book that deals most explicitly with suffering as "problem" ironically derides the answers of the wise men who come to comfort Job, the actual sufferer. In the end, God himself speaks, and instead of resolving the problem and answering the question, simply states forcefully that there is really no answer to suffering regarded as a problem. He says equivalently that man himself is the problem, and also that God is somehow central to the fact that man is man's own problem. But nothing further is explained—least of all by Job's "happy ending."

As to the ethic of the Bible: perhaps in this respect the Confucian classics are consistently clearer and more helpful than the Bible, for they present us with a coherent, easily understandable ethical system. In the Bible, on the other hand, we are constantly running into what we regard

as difficult moral problems just because of the
fact that so many of the texts, dating from different periods of human development, do not
harmonize easily. Abraham, cited by St. Paul as
the model of our belief ·and obedience to God,
was on the point of solemnizing a human sacrifice
of his firstborn—a practice that did not meet with
much approval from the prophets. Many of those
whom the Old Testament praises as being "according to God's own heart" did things which
would not agree with our ethical standards. We
must not be surprised or shocked that a certain
amount of brutality, trickery, and crude oppor-
tunism are sometimes numbered among the "qualities" of Biblical heroes in the more ancient docu-
ments.

We do not have to resort to the casuistical
gymnastics by which Augustine seeks to excuse
the lies of the Patriarch Jacob and to prove that
he was really telling the truth on some other very
obscure level. Jacob lied to his father and to his
brother, and that was part of the archaic story
whose point was not that Jacob was a truthful
man but that he transmitted the blessing and
inheritance of the fathers to his children. The
question is not one of proper behavior but of
legal *identity:* the identity of the chosen people,
the heirs of the blessing and promise of Abraham,
according to a very primitive and archaic concept
of legality.

Thus we have to be perfectly clear about what to expect in the Bible. We do not go looking for metaphysical insights into the ground of reality, moral insights into the ethics of every possible human act, still less methods of contemplative discipline or of self-transcendence by trance states and mystic illumination. Nor do we go looking for theological and philosophical systems and articulate explanations of how the universe works. Those in the past who came to understand the Biblical cosmogony as a substitute for scientific knowledge ran into immense difficulties, and their errors of judgment were great enough to be a permanent humiliation for their spiritual descendants.

In the long run, every attempt to find in the Bible what is not clearly there leads to a one-sided reading of the sacred books and ultimately to distorted and erroneous vision. This is the kind of thing that has ended by making so many modern men suspicious of the Bible, so that even believers are sometimes afraid to get involved in it. But there should be fewer problems if we would simply read what is *there*, even with its many-sided, perhaps confusing, view of things. To accept the Bible in its *wholeness* is not easy. We are much more inclined to narrow it down to a one-track interpretation which actually embraces only a very limited aspect of it. And we dignify that one-track view with the term "faith." Actu-

ally it is the opposite of faith: it is an escape from
the mature responsibility of faith which plunges
into the many-dimensional, the paradoxical, the
conflicting elements of the Bible as well as those
of life itself, and finds unity not by *excluding* all
it does not understand but by *embracing and
accepting* things in their often disconcerting reality.

We must not therefore open the Bible with
any set determination to reduce it to the limits of
a preconceived pattern of our own. And in reading
it we must not succumb to the temptation of short-
cuts and half-truths. All attempts to narrow the
Bible down until it fits conveniently into the slots
prepared for it by our prejudice will end with
our misunderstanding the Bible and even falsifying
its truth.

This will unfortunately be the case even if
our prejudices happen to be religious ones. The
history of Biblical interpretation shows how easy
it is to apply reductionist tactics to the religious
understanding of the Bible: taking the immensely
varied contents of the different books and mould-
ing them together in set simplistic forms which are
all the easier to manipulate in that they ignore
the real difficulties involved. Whenever a serious
problem arises, it can be evaded by sleight of
hand, the literal sense magically transformed into
something else.

This was perhaps forgivable in ages less
equipped than our own to cope with the technical

problems of Scripture. Indeed the allegories of medieval and patristic interpretation have a creative value of their own and often arrive at astonishing insights by roundabout ways. But allegorism is not the only way of reducing the Bible to a set of simple patterns that tell us what we want to hear. It is just as easy to do this in the name of scientific criticism, concentrating upon external detail and ignoring the inner meaning of the text. Not only that, but even such a sophisticated scholar as Bultmann is open to the accusation of "reductionism" if he is understood to mean that by *removing myth* one can arrive at a basic and pure essence of Christianity in the Bible. (I am not so sure that Bultmann really means this, however!)

In reading the Bible, we have to be quite objective and realistic in seeking out the actual meaning intended by the authors of each text. This means also taking into account their use of myth, which is to be *in*cluded, not *ex*cluded. Yet at the same time we cannot disregard the fact that the book has come to be a unified whole and, by the time the canon was completed, was clearly read as such. We must at the same time respect the wide variety of literary forms and historical backgrounds, which give special characters to the separate books, and yet remember that the Bible as a whole can and should be seen as imparting a unified, or unifiable, theological message. To do this is perhaps inevitably to bring in something external to the Bible, namely, Tradition; but whatever one may think about that, the fact is that the book is the work not only of many writers but also of many editors, whose intentions must also be taken into account along with those of the authors, for to *edit* is also to *interpret*.

Whether or not the reader is capable of theological faith in the Bible as "the word of God," and whether or not he is able to find any meaning at all in the notion of faith, he cannot begin to understand the Bible unless he agrees to accept something that was obviously in the minds of the authors and the editors alike: the belief that through the Biblical text there comes an inner content which challenges the reader and demands of him a personal engagement, a decision and commitment of his freedom, a judgment regarding an ultimate question.

This, as Bultmann has shown, requires two levels of understanding: first, a preliminary un-ravelling of the meaning of the texts themselves, a *Vorverständnis*, which is mainly a matter of knowledge acquired by study; then a deeper level, a living insight which grows out of personal involvement and relatedness: *Lebensverhältnis*. Only on this second level is the Bible really grasped, and it is to this deeper level (not necessarily "mystical" or obscure, but certainly personal) that the writers and editors of the Biblical canon obviously addressed themselves.

Unfortunately the historico-critical method, which is necessary for the first level, the "preliminary knowledge," cannot offer all the comprehension which belongs to the second level, for which it is no more than a preparation. Too often the preparatory work is taken for the final meaning, and the passage to personal relatedness and insight is never made. As a result, the Bible can seem to be poor stuff indeed, with little to recommend it except that it is sometimes colorful, sometimes bizarre, sometimes lively and fresh, sometimes even touching. But it will remain curiously alien to us if we do not make contact, by living commitment, with the challenging word that is addressed to us, the word that is, in the expression of James (1:21) "planted in us as a living seed."

It now remains for us to consider the dynamism of germination and growth which takes place when one receives and understands this "living seed." In doing so, we will avoid technical theology and simply concentrate on the way *any* serious reading of the Bible, even if only as literature, does something to the one who reads it.

What is said here should be true not only when one "has faith" (theological) in the Bible but also when one simply engages in reading the Bible with that "willing suspension of disbelief" which is usually necessary if one is to enjoy a creative work. In other words, even when one does not "believe in" the Bible as the word of God, if he takes the book at all seriously he will find that it brings us into direct confrontation with the basic problems of life. Of course, some apologists have overdone this approach to the Bible. They have exploited its challenge as an *accusation* in order to make man feel guilty and afraid, to increase his dissatisfaction with himself, to unsettle him, to make him wonder if he needs to go to church.

Bonhoeffer has criticized this approach rather scathingly, and the resulting "secular Christianity" has tended to deride that personal and existential anxiety which from St. Paul to St. Augustine, Pascal and Kierkegaard has come to be regarded as almost essential to a Christian understanding of the Bible. According to this familiar view, a serious reading of the Bible seems to imply a real crisis of anguish, conversion, and renewal. But this is too sweeping and too dramatic. Over-emphasis on this emotional aspect of it, with implications that the power of God's word is only really felt in a tragic personal upheaval, can in fact lead to subtle forms of intellectual and spiritual dishonesty.

While some people would not be true to themselves and to their own lives if they did not respond to the Bible wholly, completely, by letting themselves be overwhelmed by it, others are bound to be less excitable. They do not have it in them to go through conversion experiences except perhaps in a very slow, placid, reflective, almost unconscious sort of way. They should not be made to feel that if they have not shuddered with dread at the wrath of God they have missed the point of the Bible. Let them reflect on the Books of Wisdom rather than on the prophets, on the more serene New Testament parables rather than on the Apocalypse. In either case, whether one feels himself in a state of irremediable crisis or simply reflects that the Bible has something meaningful to say about life, the authentic response has the same basic character. Let us try to see what the Biblical experience involves.

First, we become aware that the Bible deals with *events* rather than with theories or ideas. A religious system can no doubt be built on the Bible. But the Bible message is communicated through *happenings* and is implied in the more or less explicit meaning of those happenings, for mankind, for the People of God, for us personally.

Second, these happenings all take on the character of unexpected and free *interventions or breakthroughs*. They are often explosive, astonishing, dramatic. They result from a collision of wills. In familiar language, man and God are in conflict with each other in the Bible. In more sophisticated and general terms: man as an individual or, more often, in his collective and social existence, is determined to achieve some end which is in conflict with his own inner truth, his own destiny. Man does not spontaneously agree with those deeper and more authentic possibilities which he is summoned to attain by life itself. If he refuses to pay attention to the warnings which show he is heading for disaster, he ends in a crisis situation in which he may be completely destroyed. But he may be pulled out of it unexpectedly in an undeserved rescue, through which God gives him another chance.

Third, if man simply follows his own inclinations and his own ideas, even when they appear to be good ones, he is not fully protected against error and dishonesty. He needs to be able to listen to other, more inscrutable and more direct commands, issued at the very center of his personal existence and reaching into the depths of his own identity and freedom in such a way that he "knows" they are directly intended for him personally by the ultimate Lord of life and death, Yahweh, the Nameless but wakeful and present One who is, in Augustine's phrase, more intimate to us than we are to ourselves.

Loyalty to our own inner truth and to the reality of our own lives therefore includes and demands loyalty to this *inmost* truth which is in a sense utterly beyond us. From this inmost center come imperatives which we do not naturally anticipate. From this center God grants us assistance which is absolutely necessary and yet which we cannot claim as a strict right. The Bible adds that we are congenitally inclined to doubt and disobey this deepest and most intimate imperative. There is in us a native and ongoing contest between our deepest ground and a more shallow identity which seems more familiar to us, which we are more ready to accept as "ourselves," and which we prefer to this inner and transcendent ground of freedom. But the Bible (illustrating in one event after another, whether in the history of individuals or of the People of God) teaches us that it is disastrous to prefer our more shallow self to the transcendent will that is in us yet beyond us. Even though from some points of view there is no strictly compelling reason why disaster must follow, yet it does follow, not merely because of logic but because of a special relationship between these two wills, these two freedoms:

the will of man and the "will of God." We can have no true peace and happiness except in unity, reconciliation, wholeness.

The split in man is intimately related to suffering, not so much in the sense that suffering is a penalty, but in the sense that it is a salutary incentive to change. If we did not *feel* that there was something wrong, we would do nothing to change our condition. Suffering is a symptom of disorder, and if we can understand its message, we can learn how to become once again unified and reconciled with ourselves and with God. The problem of suffering resides in our mistaken determination to *get rid of* all suffering while resolutely maintaining the division and protecting the split-off ego-self which is the focus of suffering.

Fourth, the confrontation of two conflicting freedoms and their interplay in history on two different levels is not static and arbitrary. It is an ongoing relationship which is progressive and formative, and implies a historical development of human freedom, its education and its maturing by committed interaction and engagement with the ultimate (divine) freedom. Here the notion of covenant (testament) comes in, a notion that is very important in the Bible. The covenant theme is not merely contractual, legal, in the sense that it defines strict obligations and provides sanctions that must be accepted in advance in case one violates the agreement. Essentially the idea of covenant is that of agreement, of partnership, of mutual commitment between the limited and contingent freedom of man and the ultimate, unlimited freedom of God. When the Bible says that Noah, Abraham, Moses make covenants with God, it is saying that man is the true son of God, called to share in the work of tending and using the world created by God, of participating in a work which is being carried out in history. It is saying, not that man is a slave, bound to servile and blind submission to mysterious and omnipotent power, but that he is free and able in his own right to respond or not to the freedom of God himself. In making a covenant with God, man does not alienate his freedom but affirms it. In his engagement with the freedom that guides events, man develops and perfects his own freedom.

Fifth, at this point the relationship of the two Testaments becomes clear. It is more than a matter of two convenient names. To read the whole Bible, that is to say, the Bible as understood by Christians, means to come to an understanding of the two Testaments in their relation to each other: to see how the New Testament claims to fulfill and to perfect the Abrahamic and Mosaic covenant in a completely new kind of freedom which, according to Paul, demands an emancipation even from the Law, or rather a perfection of freedom which is no longer obligated to obey the detail of the Law because it is in fact the end for which the Law was instituted.

Sixth, it is at this point that the Christian happening becomes a matter of critical importance, one on which Jews and Christians are utterly divided. The New Testament asserts that the full manifestation of God is in fact a self-emptying *(kenosis)* in which God becomes man and even submits to death at the hands of men (see Philippians 2:5-11). The word of God is now not only event but person, and the entire meaning and content of the Bible is to be found, say the Apostles, not in the message about Christ but in an encounter with Christ, who is at once person and word of God and who lives as the Risen Lord. The fulness of the Bible is, then (for Christians), the personal encounter with Christ Jesus in which one recognizes him as "the one who is sent" (the Messiah or anointed Lord, *Kyrios Christos*). He contains in himself all the questions and all the answers, all the hope and all the meanings, all the problems and all the solutions. To become utterly committed to this person and to share in the event which is his coming, his death, and his resurrection is to find the meaning of existence, not by figuring it out but by living it as he did.

The great question of the New Testament, the question which includes all others, is *who* is Christ and what does it mean to encounter him? The rest follows: *how* is one to share in this event and enter into the Christ-life, how does one participate in the existence of the Son of Man? This is not the place to treat this question in detail. Enough to say that the New Testament's answer is "in the word of the Cross," by which the shallow self, the ego-self which clings to a relatively superficial and limited freedom centered in its own satisfaction, surrenders to the ultimate Christ-self, the New Man created in justice and holiness of truth (Ephesians 4:24), in which our freedom is moved not by ego-fantasy but by the Spirit of Christ speaking out of the inmost ground of our being in our encounter with our brother. In this obedience to the Spirit of God who has now identified himself by grace with our own spirit, we reach the peak of freedom and exist entirely *for others*, no longer held back by our own petty limitations. The establishment of the kingdom of God is, then, manifested by the peace and unity of those who love one another in the Spirit. Unfortunately, even believers fail in this love, this selflessness.

We cannot enter into this dynamic of freedom and understanding unless, in reading the Bible, we somehow become aware that we are problems to ourselves. The Bible is a message of reconciliation and unity, but in order to awaken us to our need for unity it brings out the contradictions within us and makes us aware of a fundamental division.

By this painful sense of inner division we are born into the hard realities of history and severed from an unconscious, undifferentiated immersion in the womb of irresponsibility and of instinct. To be in history is to have a task and a destiny, a difficult responsibility to oneself and to others. God has called man to a freedom in which man can build for himself a world of love —or refuse to do so, and remain enmeshed in greed, hatred, lust, murder. Fromm puts it well when he says:

> Man is beset by the existential dichotomy of being within nature and yet transcending it by the fact of having self-awareness and choice; he can solve the dichotomy only by going forward. Man has to experience himself as a stranger in the world, estranged from himself and from nature, in order to become one again with himself, with his fellow man and with nature on a higher level. He has to experience the split between himself as subject and the world as object as the condition for overcoming this very split (*You Shall Be As Gods*, p. 88).

In being divided from the inmost truth which is God, or Christ living in us, we are in fact divided against what is most real and most authentic in our own selves. What is called by theological cliché "original sin" is not merely a seemingly unfair moral disability contracted for us by some pristine parent in a balmy grove: it is a spontaneous inclination to resolve the split in ourselves by denying that it exists and by closing ourselves in upon the superficial and exterior unity of the empirical ego. In other words, we affirm our unity on a shallow and provisional level by shutting out other persons and by closing off the deepest area of inner freedom where the ego is no longer in full conscious control. Thus we cheaply purchase a relative security; we contrive for ourselves an identity we think we can more easily manage and live up to.

But it is a false identity because it is only partial and does not even represent that which is authentically personal in us. Thus, cut off from our true inner selves, we remain alienated beings, semi-fictions, masks. Our best energies are wasted in playing various arbitrary roles. We fail to use our powers in being true to that which is most hidden, most unique and most demanding in the ground of our own freedom.

Society abets us in this pretense, and does so enthusiastically. It is easier for all concerned if we substitute a few introjected social norms for the inner dictates of our freedom as sons of God, or in more modern terms, if we prefer the domination of our superego to the freedom of the Holy Spirit (see Ephesians 4; Romans 8; 1 Corinthians 3; etc.).

In other words, we face a choice: on one hand we can decide to exist and function within the limitations of a partial, divided, cut-off self, protecting our own egoistic interests and adjusting these to a collective social structure in which self-interest is systematized. Or else we can respond to a "word" that breaks through this comfortable little system and shatters all its precarious selfish values, challenging us to risk a higher and more fundamental freedom. If we respond we experience a liberation from the narrowness of an ego that seeks to build its own security entirely around itself. We experience ourselves as called to participate in the revolutionary liberation of the world by the Cross. We realize ourselves as claimed by the dynamic and redemptive power of the Lord of history. We are aware of belonging to him and to his truth, and we experience his love as the driving force of our own personal life and of human history.

The central content of the Bible, what it is really about, what opens itself to the amazed understanding of one who really grasps the message, is this unique claim: THAT THE INNER TRUTH OF MAN AND OF HUMAN EXISTENCE IS

REVEALED IN A CERTAIN KIND OF EVENT. THIS
EVENT HAS THE NATURE OF *KAIROS*, CRISIS OR
JUDGMENT. CHALLENGED BY A DIRECT HISTORI-
CAL INTERVENTION OF GOD (WHICH MAY BE
DOUBTFUL AND OBSCURE BUT IS NONE THE LESS
DECISIVE), MAN CAN RESPOND WITH THE ENGAGE-
MENT OF HIS DEEPEST FREEDOM, OR HE CAN
EVADE THE ENCOUNTER BY VARIOUS SPECIOUS
EXCUSES. IF THE ENCOUNTER IS EVADED, MAN'S
FREEDOM IS NOT VINDICATED BUT IS MORTGAGED
AND FORFEITED. (But the confrontation can be
renewed in other circumstances. One may get
another chance!) WHEN THE ENCOUNTER IS REAL
AND COMPLETE, A NEW KIND OF RELATIONSHIP
IS ESTABLISHED BETWEEN OUR OWN FREEDOM
AND THAT ULTIMATE FREEDOM AND SPIRIT: THE
GOD WHO IS LOVE AND WHO IS ALSO THE "LORD
OF HISTORY." AT THE SAME TIME A NEW RELA-
TIONSHIP WITH OTHER MEN COMES INTO BEING:
INSTEAD OF LIVING FOR OURSELVES, WE LIVE FOR
THEM. IDEALLY SPEAKING, IF WE ALL LIVED IN
THIS KIND OF ALTRUISTIC CONCERN AND EN-
GAGEMENT, HUMAN HISTORY WOULD CULMINATE
IN AN EPIPHANY OF GOD IN MAN. MANKIND
WOULD VISIBLY BE "CHRIST."

It will be seen from this that the Bible is
concerned with something far deeper than the
establishment of a religious system. In fact, the
Bible is in some sense far more than a "religious"

book. Karl Barth long ago pointed out the basic tension between faith and "religion" in the Bible.

What is meant by "religion"? The dutiful cult of a Supreme Being, a Highest Good, who is acknowledged in suitably reverent worship, honored by ritual sacrifices, appeased by propitiatory gestures or penances, and petitioned in humble prayer. Luther defined a "religious act" in this sense as one in which the worshipper reassures himself by saying "If I do this, God will be clement to me," and he contrasted this human form of expression in religious works with the faith which is directly awakened in us by confrontation with God in the nakedness and confusion of sin.

Bultmann defines religion in terms of "redemption myths" and the quest for a refuge in eternity. It is "man's yearning for something beyond this world, the discovery of a sphere above the world in which only the soul can live, detaching itself from worldly things. In religion man is alone with God . . . . Religion shows itself not in the shaping of the life of the world but in the aimless action of the cultus" (*Kerygma and Myth*, I, 14).

Clearly this is a more hellenistic view which is alien to the Bible, though the Bible has come to be interpreted in this sense. But obviously the Bible has more to do than address itself to "the soul" and prescribe sure-fire methods for individual rescue from the world. The Bible is very much concerned with the world and with all who are in it, and most of its books are clearly not oriented to "the great beyond," but to God present in his world. As Bonhoeffer says: "The Beyond is not infinitely remote but close at hand." The Bible acknowledges no permanent chasm between man and God and does not seek to bridge the gulf by mere religious acts. On the contrary, the reconciliation of man with God is seen in more deeply mysterious and existential terms as a spiritual identification in pardon, sonship, grace, freedom, love and community. And here religious acts tend to lose their meaning as signals across an infinite abyss or as efficacious means for propitiating an utterly remote Power and gaining his support in our worldly political ventures. To say that the Bible goes beyond religion is to say that it preaches the *kenosis* or self-emptying of God and his identification of himself with man as person and as community, in Christ.

Hence though there are many trends in the Bible which reflect a high degree of ritualism and religiosity, we also find that systematically organized "religion" is sometimes questioned by the Bible, particularly by the prophets and by the New Testament writers. The whole struggle of Christ with the Jewish establishment over sabbath observance was in fact a struggle over religious practices; and the pharisees, as sincerely religious men, were right in their own way to be frightened and scandalized by the revolutionary preaching in which Christ affirmed that his new way would imply an entirely new understanding of worship (Matthew 6:1-18; 15:1-20; etc.).

But it would be entirely wrong, a complete misunderstanding of the Bible, to interpret this in a shallow way, as liberal Christianity might do, asserting that the ultimate fruit of the New Testament is merely a kind of polite scepticism and a bland religious indifference which tolerates any and every kind of conduct provided there is "good will" and "you don't hurt others." We have seen that the radical insight of a film director like Pasolini could bring out the absolutism and intransigence of the Gospel Jesus, who was not mild and tolerant but extremely demanding.

In a way the demands of Christ are much more ruthless than those of the Torah. He is in no sense *anti-religious*. He does not come to destroy the religious law but to go beyond it and fulfil it (Matthew 5:17-19). He does so because his view is entirely eschatological: it foresees the imminent end of the kind of society in which an archaic religious practice is relevant. In other words, Jesus foresees the end of a world that is fragmented and divided, and in which each division or fragment asserts its identity by special rites in honor of a special god. The God to whom the "religious" man cries as "My God" has hitherto been the God of his tribe, his nation, his king.

Hence the "My God" of tribal or national religion is by definition not "their God"—he is *for* us and *against* everyone else. If "religion" merely exists in order to establish this peculiar emphasis on one's collective identity, then it is indeed rendered obsolete by the universalism of the prophets and of the apostles.

Religion in this sense is gradually revealed in the Bible to be under judgment. It is questioned not so much by man *as by God himself.* One of the most drastic affirmations of the New Testament (and indeed of the Old) is that it foresees a time in which religion itself is purged away! Hence the burning issue of the Temple. Jesus was crucified on the charge, among others, of plotting to destroy the Temple. Stephen was stoned to death for declaring the Temple henceforth obsolete (Acts 7:48-53). The eschatology of the New Testament, and indeed that of the prophets and apocalypses, is extremely severe in regard to any kind of "religion" that, on the pretext of mediating between man and God, in effect sets itself up as a substitute for God and as a barrier between man and man, as we see clearly, for example, in Isaiah:

> Hear the word of the Lord, you rulers of Sodom! Give ear to the teaching of our God, you people of Gomorrah! "What to me is the multitude of your sacrifices? says the Lord. I have had enough of burnt offerings

of rams and the fat of fed beasts. I do not
delight in the blood of bulls, or of lambs or
of he-goats. When you come to appear before me, who requires of you this trampling
of my courts? Bring no more vain offerings;
incense is an abomination to me. New moon
and sabbath and the calling of assemblies—
I cannot endure iniquity and solemn assem-
bly. Your new moons and your appointed
feasts my soul hates; they have become a
burden to me, I am weary of bearing them.
When you spread forth your hands, I will
hide my eyes from you; even though you
make many prayers, I will not listen; your
hands are full of blood" (Isaiah 1:10-15).

Here, of course, religious worship is not condemn-
ed and rejected as such, but only in so far as it is
an external formality and a façade for exclusive-
ness, cruelty and injustice. But for St. Paul, clearly the Christian who has "died with Christ" is
liberated from merely human religious obligations,
ritual customs, taboos, dietary prohibitions, or
gnostic contemplations, based on adherence to a
special "pure" and "chosen" group.

See to it that no one makes a prey of you
by philosophy and empty deceit, according
to human tradition, according to the elemental spirits of the universe, and not according to Christ. ... Therefore let no one
pass judgment on you in questions of food
and drink or with regard to a festival or a
new moon or a sabbath. These are only a

shadow of what is to come; but the substance belongs to Christ. Let no one disqualify you, insisting on self-abasement and worship of angels, taking his stand on visions, puffed up without reason by his sensuous mind, and not holding fast to the Head, from whom the whole body, nourished and knit together through its joints and ligaments, grows with a growth that is from God. If with Christ you died to the elemental spirits of the universe, why do you live as if you still belonged to the world? Why do you submit to regulations, "Do not handle, Do not taste, Do not touch" [referring to things which all perish as they are used], according to human precepts and doctrines? (Colossians 2:8, 16-22).

Even the most extraordinary moral heroism and charismatic gifts cannot substitute, in Paul's eyes, for the essential thing which is love (see 1 Corinthians 13:1-13).

The question of "religionless Christianity" raised by radical theologians today is therefore more than mere sensationalism. It *does* have a basis in the Bible. But this does not mean that every new report from God-is-dead land is to be taken as final. On the contrary, those among the new theologians who can be trusted are simply raising new and difficult questions which will not be answered until there has been a much more thoughtful investigation. Let it suffice to be clear that Bonhoeffer did *not* mean that true Christianity was religionless, or anti-religious. Or if he did, the idea was put forward as a hypothesis rather than as a dogma. But the point is that the serious questioning and criticism of "religion," "the religious instinct," and "religious experience" *have a firm basis in the Bible.* where we know that God judges the righteous first of all, and judgment begins with the sanctuary of the Lord (Ezekiel 9:6).

☆ ☆ ☆

Real understanding of the Bible demands a constant alert openness to all the different dynamic elements that work together, all the different trends, materials, literary forms, viewpoints in both Testaments. On one hand there are religious, ritualistic, priestly elements; on the other, prophetic, iconoclastic and anti-establishment trends. There is a royalist, urban, national theme. There are the scribes, the wise men, with their prudential and down-to-earth teaching. There are the apocalyptic writers with their vision of an ultimate reckoning. Then there are the apostles, seeing in Christ the fulfilment of all revealed promises, the ultimate focus of reconciliation between men and God, drawing together in him all the combined messages and teachings of the law and the prophets.

As the Bible progresses, we get an ever growing sense of the urgency and meaning of time, of man's history. We get a sense of *kairos*, of an ultimate "time" foreseen and foretold by God, a moment of breakthrough toward which history itself, with all the good and evil that are in man, has gradually been maturing.

In this "last age" all the struggles and problems of man come to a head, and he faces extraordinary decisions upon which rest not only the fate of individuals but the judgment of nations and of the human race itself. In this time of great crisis, everything in man, including all he holds most sacred, must come under scrutiny and under judgment. All his institutions, his aspirations, his hopes and desires are weighed and estimated in terms of *love*. If they are seen to be under the "wrath of God," it is because they are evil, because they have become opaque and deceptive, frustrating the ends which they promise to fulfil, dividing men in hatred and mutual exploitation instead of uniting them in love and peace.

When the living relationship with God hardens into a rigid and "established system" that claims to give man full control of all the answers and encourages him to "use" even God for his own purposes, then nature and culture, law and religion and even prophecy become ambiguous, deceptive, fatal not only to man but to man's ability to apprehend the truth of God. In such a situation, the most sacred and fundamental conceptions become meaningless and it is said that "God is dead" because man has lost the capacity to find any real sense or hope in what should be the message of ultimate joy and realization. It is then, especially, that culture, the state, even the religious establishment, are said to be "under the wrath of God." All the more so when it becomes impossible to conceive just what God and his wrath could possibly mean. At such a time, the capacity for *openness*, the ability to listen to the word of God and hear it, becomes a precious and paradoxical gift: for the word will make itself heard in the most unexpected places. And it may tend to be understood by the people you would be least inclined to qualify as "religious."

The *kairos*, the special, critical time, is then not only a time of breakthrough, convergence, the destruction of the old, the invasion by the new and unforeseen—it is above all *a time of decisive response*.

It would seem that we live in such a time. Our response will depend not on deftly picking up and appropriating the latest answers, the most novel explanations, but on our ability to accept ourselves and our time as highly problematic. It will depend on our openness to the future, the unpredictable, the disconcerting.

We are on the threshold of a new age. The Bible does not necessarily spell out what we can expect to find when we cross the threshold, but it does reveal to us the *basic dynamism* of human existence under God, a dynamism of awareness and response, in which lies "salvation." The rest is a matter of "believe and you will understand."